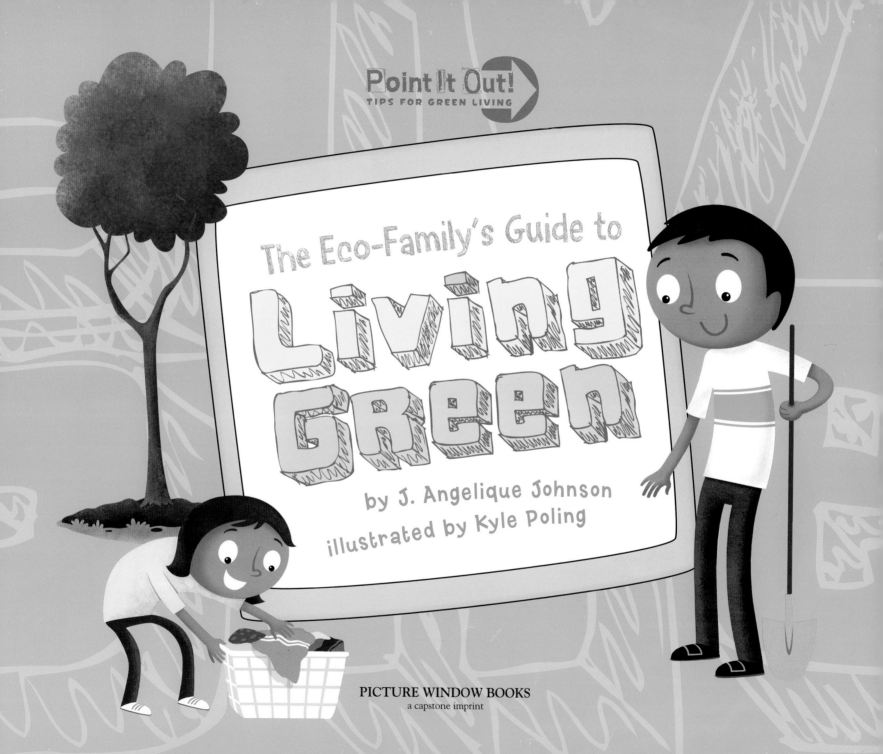

Point It Out!
TIPS FOR GREEN LIVING

The Eco-Family's Guide to

Living Green

by J. Angelique Johnson

illustrated by Kyle Poling

PICTURE WINDOW BOOKS
a capstone imprint

It seems everyone is "going green." But do you know what living green really means? It means finding ways to keep our surroundings clean and healthy. These places include our world, communities, schools, and homes. Living green also means making healthful choices for our bodies and the bodies of others.

Check out ways you can live green by looking closely at the rooms on the pages throughout this book.

Oh, No!

The heat from the lamp tells the thermostat the room temperature is hotter than it really is. Move the lamp away from the thermostat. You'll save energy by lowering the heat.

Way to Go!

You have a laptop instead of a desktop computer. A laptop uses only one-fourth of the energy a desktop computer uses.

Oh, No!

You left the computer on. Most computers have a "sleep" mode to save energy. Learn how to put your computer to sleep, or turn it off.

Way to Go!

Use power strips to plug in the computer and monitor. To save energy, switch off the strip when these items aren't in use.

Did You Know...

FOR EVERY DEGREE YOU LOWER YOUR THERMOSTAT, YOUR FAMILY WILL SAVE 3 TO 5% ON HEATING COSTS.

Did You Know...

YOU CAN SAVE ENERGY BY REPLACING LIGHTBULBS WITH ENERGY STAR BULBS. THESE LIGHTBULBS USE UP TO 75% LESS ENERGY THAN OTHER BULBS.

Way to Go!

You're using a small lamp for reading. Save energy by using task lighting when reading.

Oh, No!

Don't let old clothes pile up on your floor or go to waste. Put items you've outgrown to good use. Donate them to a thrift store.

11

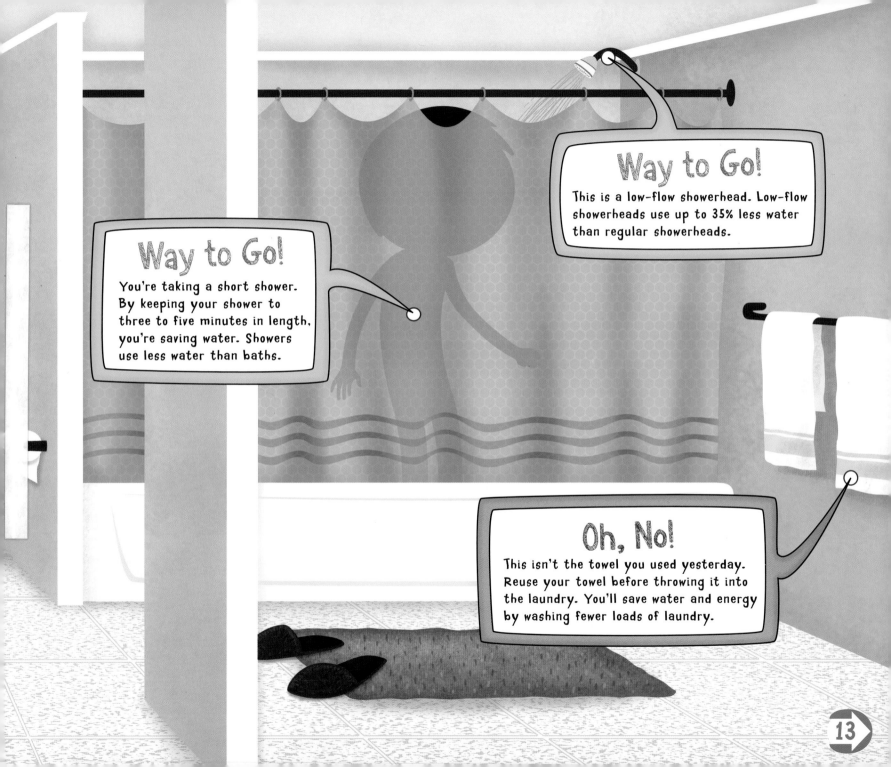

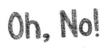

Oh, No!

Ask adults to avoid chlorine bleach. They can use a hydrogen peroxide-based bleach instead. It's safe for people and the environment.

BLEACH

CAT FOOD

CAT FOOD

Way to Go!

You have enough for a full load. Washing a full load of clothes saves water and energy.

Way to Go!

You're washing that load in cold water. Using cold water to wash clothes saves energy and doesn't fade colors.

Oh, No!

The dryer has been running for a long time. You can dry clothes on a line to save energy. If you use a dryer, run it only as long as necessary.

Oh, No!

Don't use oil-based paint! Oil-based paint contains high levels of volatile organic compounds (VOCs). VOCs are bad for the environment. VOCs can also make people feel sick. Instead, ask for low-VOC or no-VOC paints at your local home store.

Way to Go!

This is a bamboo floor. Bamboo is a type of hard grass that grows quickly. It makes great flooring without hurting the environment.

Way to Go!

Driving an energy-efficient car saves gas. It also produces fewer emissions. To save even more gas, think ahead, and plan your family's errands into one large trip.

Oh, No!

Don't bag your groceries in plastic bags. Plastic bags don't break down quickly in landfills. It's best to use cotton totes when you shop. But if you choose plastic bags, return them to the store. You can also find a way to reuse them.

Did You Know...

YOU CAN HELP SAVE GAS BY REMINDING ADULTS TO REPAIR ENGINES, REPLACE AIR FILTERS, AND PROPERLY INFLATE TIRES.

Way to Go!
Your clothes are on the line. Limit dryer use, and save energy by hanging clothes outdoors to dry.

Oh, No!
Don't leave that hose running. Turn off the nozzle to save water.

Living green means knowing about our resources. Some resources, such as wind power, are renewable. That means they most likely will never go away, no matter how much of them we use. Other resources, such as oil, are limited. We must be careful how much of these resources we use.

By living green at home, you can help save Earth's resources. You can make Earth and your own home clean, healthy places to live. Take a look around your home. How can you make it "green"?

Glossary

chlorine—a harmful chemical used in bleach; it is also used to clean water

compost—a mixture of dead leaves, grass clippings, and even kitchen scraps that are mixed together to make fertilizer

efficient—not being wasteful

emissions—gases released into the air, often poisonous

environment—everything surrounding people, animals, and plants

hydrogen peroxide—a colorless chemical used in some bleaches, cosmetics, and medicines

insulation—a kind of material put into walls to protect a house from losing heat

landfill—land set aside where garbage is dumped and buried

organic—grown without the use of chemicals

resources—wind, sunlight, soil, water, and/or animals are all examples of resources

thermostat—a device that controls indoor temperature

volatile organic compounds (VOCs)—chemicals that change quickly from liquid to vapor; they pollute the air and are harmful to humans

To Learn More

More Books to Read

Hewitt, Sally. *Your Food*. Green Team. New York: Crabtree Pub. Co., 2009.

Nelson, Sara Elizabeth. *Let's Reuse!* Caring for the Earth. Mankato, Minn.: Capstone Press, 2007.

Orme, Helen. *Living Green*. Earth in Danger. New York: Bearport Pub., 2009.

Internet Sites

FactHound offers a safe, fun way to find Internet sites related to this book. All of the sites on FactHound have been researched by our staff.

Here's all you do:
Visit *www.facthound.com*
Type in this code: 9781404860261

Index

Look for all of the books in the Point It Out! Tips for Green Living series:

The Eco-Family's Guide to Living Green
The Eco-Neighbor's Guide to a Green Community
The Eco-Shopper's Guide to Buying Green
The Eco-Student's Guide to Being Green at School

Special thanks to our advisers for their expertise:

Rebecca Meyer, Extension Educator
4-H Youth Development
University of Minnesota Extension, Cloquet

Terry Flaherty, Ph.D., Professor of English
Minnesota State University, Mankato

Editor: Shelly Lyons
Designer: Alison Thiele
Art Director: Nathan Gassman
Production Specialist: Jane Klenk

The illustrations in this book were created digitally.
Photo Credit: Shutterstock/Doodle, 22

Picture Window Books
151 Good Counsel Drive
P.O. Box 669
Mankato, MN 56002-0669
877-845-8392
www.capstonepub.com

Printed in the United States of America, North Mankato,
Minnesota. 032010   005740CGF10

 All books published by Picture Window Books
are manufactured with paper containing at least
10 percent post-consumer waste.

Library of Congress Cataloging-in-Publication Data
Johnson, J. Angelique.
 The eco-family's guide to living green / by J. Angelique
Johnson, illustrated by Kyle Poling.
     p. cm. — (Point it out! tips for green living)
  Includes index.
  ISBN 978-1-4048-6026-1 (library binding)
  1. Sustainable living—Juvenile literature.
2. Environmentalism—Juvenile literature. 3. Green
movement—Juvenile literature. I. Poling, Kyle. II. Title.
  GE196.J65 2010
  640—dc22
                                        2010009882